SOLITARY SPIRITS
COUGARS

NorthWord
WILDLIFE SERIES

Photography © 1996: Michael H. Francis, Cover, 47, 132-133; John Shaw, 1, 27, 42, 53, 55, 60, 77, 116-117; Brian Parker/Tom Stack & Associates, 4; Jim Dutcher/Dutcher Film Productions, 6, 28-29, 39, 45, 48-49, 56-57, 71, 78-79, 90, 101, 103, 106, 108-109, 111, 118, 122-123, 125; Richard Day/Daybreak Imagery, 8-9, 18, 36, Back cover; Art Wolfe, 10, 25, 69, 74, 81, 82, 85, 86-87, 88; Tom & Pat Leeson, 13, 30, 35, 128, 138; Dominique Braud/Dembinsky Photo Associates, 15, 134; Bill Lea/Dembinsky Photo Associates, 16-17; Lynn M. Stone, 21, 93, 95, 131; Jim Roetzel/Dembinsky Photo Associates, 22, 99, 137; D. Robert Franz/The Wildlife Collection, 32-33, 59; Tom Brakefield/Bruce Coleman, Inc., 40-41, 104-105, 112-113; Thomas Kitchin/Tom Stack & Associates, 50; Mark J. Thomas/Dembinsky Photo Associates, 63; Lorri Franz/The Wildlife Collection, 64; John S. Botkin/Dembinsky Photo Associates, 67; Frans Lanting/Minden Pictures, 72-73, 121; Gerald & Buff Corsi/Tom Stack & Associates, 96-97; Michael H. Francis/The Wildlife Collection, 115; Joe McDonald/Bruce Coleman, Inc., 126-127; Bruce Montagne/Dembinsky Photo Associates, 141; Alan & Sandy Carey, 142-143.

NorthWord Press, Inc.
P.O. Box 1360
Minocqua, WI 54548

Book design by Amy J. Monday

For a free catalog describing our audio products, nature books and calendars, call **1-800-356-4465**, or write Consumer Inquiries, NorthWord Press, Inc., P.O. Box 1360, Minocqua, Wisconsin 54548.

Library of Congress Cataloging-in-Publication Data

Olson, Dennis L.
      Cougars : solitary spirits / by Dennis L. Olson.
         p.   cm.—(Wildlife Series)
      ISBN 1-55971-574-X (pbk.)
       1. Pumas.   I. Title.   II. Series: Wildlife series
   QL737.C23O58 1996
      599.74'428—dc20   96-13258

Printed in Singapore

SOLITARY SPIRITS
COUGARS

by Dennis L. Olson

NorthWord®

NORTHWORD PRESS, INC.
Minocqua, Wisconsin

Dedication

For Mom and Dad,

Always There. . .

Acknowledgments

We are a cooperative species. This axiom is brutally obvious to a writer, especially when he or she tackles a complex project. I owe debts of gratitude to many who helped me gather knowledge of and appreciation for cougars. Gary Power, a friend, co-worker and scientist, gave me glimpses into the lives of cougars which animated his wealth of scientific information. John Beecham recalled for me his cougar days with infectious relish. Maurice Hornocker, "Mr. Cougar" to anyone familiar with wildlife research, was an inspiration. Allen Anderson and Kevin Hansen contributed immensely. "Doc" Richard Smith filled in many gaps with his anecdotes.

Less cougar-specific inspiration comes from my kids, Jesse and Kya, who often make me laugh with their great humor and joy about life. I am very lucky to have some connection with their spirits. Native peoples from ages past had relatives called cougars, and their stories are a shaping force in my life. Dana Wetzel is cougar personified, but with a sense of humor. And the NorthWord Press staff has a creative synergy with which I always enjoy participating.

Table of Contents

Left: A cougar's survival depends on investigating anything unusual.

Following pages: Hunt, eat and rest—the cougar cycle.

Introduction

My hair was marching forward on my head. It seemed like I could smell the acrid odor of adrenaline pouring from every pore in my body. The cougar's eyes were blazing in the reflected glare of my flashlight. Here I was, still two miles from the truck, with a fresh quarter of elk on my back. I kept thinking of my cats at home, how they sat coiled, pointed like a gunsight at the birds near the feeder, tails twitching. I remembered how they made their decision to spring based on only two criteria—did the prey move, and was it of suitable size? Here, I was both.

It was above me on the slope, and slightly behind, the classic stalk position of the cougar. I knew it would rush in giant leaps; each time it landed it would make a directional adjustment as I tried to wheel and dodge and run. The last leap would accomplish three things—it would knock me flat, the front claws would close around my body, and the bite at the back of my neck would be powerful and instant. My neck vertebrae would separate, pithing me like an experimental frog. Beyond my present fear, I wouldn't feel a thing.

I almost left my skin behind when the "cougar" snorted, wheeled and showed a white rump as its hooves pounded up the ridge and away.

Of course, I had seen the "cougar" (instead of the mule deer it magically transformed itself into) because of my expectations and the cumulative imaginings of a dark night in wild country. From far back in my

Patrolling for prey in a large home range demands
that miles be traveled each day.

11

own genetic mists, I had still remembered what it was like to be prey.

Part of the fear of big cats comes from our lore about man-eating tigers and African lions. Part comes from watching our own cats, Tabby and Garfield, how they kill birds, squirrels and mice utterly without a shred of remorse. Cats are killing machines, ruled by programmed behavior, physically coordinated and powerful beyond the perception of most humans, and honed by fifty million years of evolutionary practice, trial, and error.

It is easy to carelessly extrapolate from one species to another, to assume an aggressive attitude in cougars from watching domestic cats and the hair-raising bluff charges of African lions. It is especially easy to confer our preconceived ideas on the cougar, because, above all, it is an animal of mystery. It is a loner, nocturnal, living in the most remote wilderness still remaining on this planet. Its stalking skills can easily be interpreted as "sneaky." Its natural shyness can be thought of as slyness or cunning behavior. It kills quickly, powerfully, without warning.

All of our science, our urbanity, our vestigial pioneer ethic, teaches us to attack the concept of mystery with the passion of an evangelical crusade. To know facts is to pretend at dominion. We hate the idea that secrets remain everywhere. The cougar is a walking enigma, a paradox in our world, full of the illusion of control. In the past, it hasn't so much been the cougar which needed killing—it was what the cougar represented. Unfortunately, we couldn't eliminate mystery, so the large predators—the wolf, the grizzly bear, and the cougar—had to do.

Of course, this ethic of dominion is rapidly changing in our world. Two-hundred-year efforts at civilizing the land have slowed. We are conserving and even reintroducing wolves and bears to where they once belonged. We look for the wildness within ourselves by "running with wolves" or "bearwalking." But always, out there, in the dark, solitary, has been the cougar.

Perhaps it will always be difficult for us to identify with an animal as non-social as the cougar. Stealth and solitude are low on the list of desirable human traits. Name one colloquialism in our language which uses the cougar as its object: the wolf is at the door; waiting to wolf down some food; and we have all been hungry or mad as a bear. But where is the cougar in us?

The reason? We just don't know much about cougars.

The solitary hunter.

Another paradox: the very traits which make the cougar hard to emulate are the traits which have kept it from becoming as endangered as wolves and grizzly bears. As the west was being won, it was hard to civilize what you couldn't find. Without the aid of well-trained dogs, cougar hunting was, and is, virtually impossible. Except for the Florida and Eastern subspecies of cougars, their populations are healthy and increasing.

I live in prime cougar country. Even here, the passing of a cougar over the crest of a ridge will almost always be unseen and unheard, even by the elk and deer that have the most at stake. A cougar drifting by must be *felt* as much as sensed in obvious ways. The prickle you feel on your neck one day is manifest as cougar tracks the next. How an animal as magnificent and imposing as the cougar can remain a riddle in our probing world is a question about the cougar itself.

This book is about those fragments of cougar life we do know, or at least can guess at. It may seem as though we know more than we think. But clearly we know less than we pretend. To appreciate the cougar, we must understand that "mysterious" is more a synonym than an adjective.

Above: Cougars don't perspire, so panting becomes a way of regulating heat.

Following pages: Since they are primarily visual hunters, cougars often rest on a good vantage point.

Cougar Mystique.

It is only proper that an animal shrouded in mystery would have many aliases. Most Native American languages had their own name for the big cat. It is interesting that most of those names deified the cougar, calling it a lord or a cat from God. While most western names didn't vilify the cougar, the actions of European settlers were anything but reverent. The earliest European settlers, primarily from Spain, were quite confident that they were seeing lions, of the African variety. Since new names usually come from an old frame of reference, it is not surprising that "tiger" and "panther" were also common names for the big American cat. "Panther," another name for the African leopard, is still used today. "Lion" was amended to "mountain lion," but that name is also a misnomer, because cougars live many places other than the mountains. "Painter" is also heard in southern and eastern North America. It is a probably a drawl mispronunciation of panther. New England folks, always fiercely independent, came up with another mountain misnomer, the "catamount."

The western names of cougar and puma both originated in the southern hemisphere. "Cougar" is shortened from a name by a tribe in the Brazilian rain forest. "Puma" comes from the Incas, and loosely translated means "magic mighty animal."

The latter two names don't inadvertently pass misinformation and

Cougars need cover dense enough for hiding yet sparse enough for silent stalking.

are unique to *Felis concolor*, but of the two, "cougar" is the most widely known. For that reason, this book uses the name cougar.

Legends and Lore

The outer edge of cougar country borders the places yet to be populated. It wasn't always that way. Once, the path of the cougar was traveled by the First Americans—literally and figuratively. Hunter societies in the Southwest pueblos carried small stone fetishes of the cougar during deer hunts, being careful to share the kill with the spirit of the cougar. They were mindful that the leftovers from cougar kills were an important food source for their human ancestors. Warrior societies were sometimes named after the cougar, and entrance into the society was contingent on the ceremonial killing of one. If a warrior was successful at killing a cougar on its own terms, it was not a statement on the prowess of the human hunter. To the warrior, the cougar had made the choice. The warrior had been humble enough, had learned enough of the stalking and escape skills of the cougar, and had approached the cougar with the proper level of respect. He had earned the paws he now carried around his neck.

Cougars are hardly ever the main character in traditional Native American stories. Perhaps it is because the big cat is so secretive—it appeared rarely even to those who lived in the wild. In general, Native Americans had a deeper appreciation for unspoken silence, and it could be that silence about cougars was the proper way to treat such a powerful and secretive animal. The cougar is, after all, silent itself most of the time. The only sure way to not offend the spirit of the cougar was to not mention it.

So many Native American stories have been permanently lost in the last hundred years, it is likely some cougar stories disappeared as well. Another possibility is that some cougar stories are told only in the context of a ceremony, and are secret except when that ceremony is being performed.

The Seneca have a story about a young man who had a contest with his friend, to see who could hold his breath longest in a deep lake. While holding the edge of a flat rock he had found under water, a strange blue-gray man approached him and invited him deeper, to his

The Florida panther is a rare and distinctive sub-species of the cougar.

Cougars are good swimmers. Crossing a body of water may be the most efficient way to a new hunting area.

village. The young man was not frightened and followed him there. A medicine man with a strange tawny gold face and body and a pink nose was there, addressing the people. "We and the humans in the upper world are brothers. Why shouldn't we warn them of disasters to come?" he asked. The blue man volunteered for the job, and asked the young man to watch over his lodge while he was away. He was gone for four moons and finally came back looking forlorn. The blue man explained that during his visit to the upper world, he discovered that he was both a messenger and a bringer of death. When the young man returned to his village in the upper world, everyone was afraid of him at first—they thought he had died in the water months ago. The village had experienced fires, floods, disease, and starvation, and only a few of the villagers were left. When they explained that a blue cougar had appeared before all this had happened, the young man finally realized the dual nature of the blue man he came to know in the water. He taught his remaining relatives to offer tobacco to the cougar when it was seen. It would then be satisfied and return to the lake. The ambivalence native people felt toward an animal which could kill them, and yet left food behind for them most of the time, is reflected in this story.

In the northern lake country, the Ojibwe people offered Mizhipizhu, the great water panther, tobacco before they embarked on a long journey across the water. Mizhipizhu could unexpectedly whip the lake into a froth and take the lives of the disrespectful. The association northern people had between the cougar and the water is a puzzle until we watch the fluid motion of the cougar, and understand that beneath the lake surface is a place as mysterious as the cougar itself.

The White River Ute have a story which shows they have a good grasp of cougar behavior. At the Bear Dance, Bear was singing in a beautiful voice. A woman began to dance fluidly and provocatively in front of Bear. He was quite taken with her, and invited her under his blanket. Her name was Cougar Woman, and she enticed Bear out of the camp—she wanted to mate with him and was very impatient. Bear refused, saying that he only mated in the spring and summer. Cougar Woman became agitated at Bear, and said that her husband, Cougar, was very strong, and would surely kill him. Bear growled and pulled up a small tree, to show Cougar Woman that he was very strong, too. He kept pulling up trees as they traveled up a mountain. When they reached the top, Bear was so intent on proving his power that he didn't notice Cougar slinking up behind him. Cougar grabbed Bear and threw him down before Bear could react, and broke Bear's neck. Cougar didn't punish his wife, because he knew that Cougar women were very unpredictable about when they wanted to mate, and he had been off hunting at that time.

Cougar females spend almost two years raising cubs, and they have no interest in mating during that time. As soon as the cubs are on their own, however, cougar females go into heat as often as every three weeks. Cougars rely on stealth, surprise and precision when they hunt. They usually break the neck of an intended victim instantly with a killing bite. Obviously, these natural history facts were well known to the Ute.

In another Ute story, Cougar discovers Coyote eating stinging ants from an anthill, grimacing and yelping as he ate. Cougar felt sorry for Coyote, and took him to a spring to show him how he hunted. They both climbed a tree and waited. Soon a herd of wild horses came to drink, and coyote wiggled a little, impatiently. Cougar told Coyote to be still and watch. After a while, a horse came under the branch, Cougar jumped down next to the horse and then onto it, biting the back of its neck and killing it. Cougar dragged it far away and hid it, so the other horses wouldn't see it. They both fed for a few days on the horse, and Coyote thought this was a whole lot better than eating ants. Cougar decided to go away on a hunt and warned Coyote not to try killing horses by himself. "The horse will surely kill you," he said. Coyote went the other direction, and came upon another coyote eating ants. He couldn't resist showing off, and took the other coyote to the tree. After a while, the horses came and Coyote jumped onto the back of one, biting it furiously on the mane. Of course, the horse spun and Coyote landed hard on the ground. The horse stomped Coyote to death. The other coyote went back to eating ants. When Cougar returned, and climbed the tree to wait, the horses came to water and immediately ran away. Cougar was suspicious that Coyote hadn't listened to him, and sure enough, found Coyote's smashed body nearby.

The natural camouflage of a cougar, both color and behavior,
is essential for success as a stalker.

The Modern Story

The exact part the cougar played in the world of each Native American nation varied, but always there was some aspect of power, grace, mystery and respect. That all changed when the new people arrived from the east. All predators were vilified, including the big cats, as (in the words of a comparatively enlightened Teddy Roosevelt) "lords of stealthy murder." Since then the story has been "cougar as enemy." Predator control, which had been naturally accomplished for a few million years by the numbers of available prey, became a popular government program. The cougar was nearly eliminated east of the Mississippi at the turn of the century. In the "civilizing" of America, a quarter million cougars have paid the price for European fear of the wild.

Tales of "devil cats" which raided human settlements in search of the innocent thread through the folklore of the settlement era. The association with the devil, as the Salem experience graphically showed, is an indictment which must be disproven. There was no assumption of innocence when something as evil and mysterious as Satan was involved.

The facts, however, paint a different picture. Cougars are certainly capable of killing humans, but normally don't. There have been literally hundreds of millions of forays by humans into cougar country. There have been tens of thousands of sightings and encounters. From these, there have been forty-one injuries and nine deaths of humans at the paws of the cougar. Two-thirds of the injuries and deaths have been children, most of them either alone or with other children. More than three-quarters of the attacking lions have been yearlings, which are usually transient and have poor hunting skills compared to adults. Cougars can be dangerous, especially to unsupervised children, but the chances of becoming a cougar victim are far less than becoming a victim of lightning, honeybees, moose, deer, pit bulls, football, snow-shoveling or crossing the street in front of your house. For some reason, we fear the true risks of being killed far less than the remote risk of becoming prey. Dying is one thing—becoming something's lunch is another.

Above: Whiskers, or vibrissae, help cougars "feel" their way through thick cover.

Following pages: When traveling, cougars pick the route least likely to produce noise.

Cougar Signs

In the past, knowing cougars has been a science of hypotheses. Secrets from fragmentary evidence were reconstructed to conclude the presence, and then the actions, of a cougar. Once the age of radio transmitters and helicopters was upon us, a lucky few could pry into the secret life of the cougar a little deeper. Most of us don't have that technology available to us, so we must go about our cougar searches the old-fashioned way. "Low-tech" as they may be, our observations may still be the keys to figuring out the complex stories of the cougar's activities, provided we watch cougar country with care.

Tracks

The first thing most of us think of as "sign" is tracks. Tracking is dependent on the keenness of our observations, but the terrain and season are also limiting factors. Snow makes it easy. Bare bedrock in the summer makes it nearly impossible. Mud makes for good track impressions, but mud patches are intermittent, even in wet climates. Lucky for us budding "scouts," the habits of cougars are not terribly seasonal, and winter tracks can be extrapolated into probable summer stories.

Male cougar tracks are fairly large, about three-and-a-half to four inches in both length and width, on the average. The largest male

Left: Walking cougars usually make clear track impressions that are easy to identify.

Following pages: Cougar tracks are wider than long and have three lobes on the rear edge of the heel pad.

cougar tracks approach six inches in width. Female tracks don't get much larger than three inches. The tracks are slightly wider than they are long. By comparison, wolf and dog tracks of the same relative size are longer than they are wide.

If the impression is good, canids (wolves, dogs, coyotes, foxes) usually show blunt toenails. Cats, however, have retractile claws and the claws won't show on tracks made on open level ground. Occasionally, cougar claw marks can be seen where they needed some extra traction, such as when they climbed a hill in loose dirt. Of course, the marks left by cougar claws are anything but dull—they appear much the same as the impression left by the point of a knife. The outside toe of a cougar track, which corresponds to our little finger or toe, is slightly smaller than the other toes. That makes it possible to determine whether it is a right or left track you are looking at.

Each track shows four toes and a heel pad. The best way to distinguish a cougar track from any other track is the shape and size of the heel pad. Compared to canid tracks, the pad is much broader and has two lobes on its front edge and three lobes on the rear edge. The lobes on the front edge do not always show, but the three on the rear usually do.

Unless a cougar is running down prey or leaving in a panic, the rear track registers almost perfectly in the front track. In other words, all an observer will see is the rear track, especially when the big cat is stalking. This "perfect walking" is typical of wild animals, which reap benefits from making only half the noise of a sloppy-walking domestic dog.

Gary Power, a cougar biologist from Idaho, described a cat he was once following. He noticed that the tracks were slightly more fuzzy-edged than usual. He followed for a few hundred yards, when suddenly the cougar "cloned" itself three ways. He had been following a female and two nearly grown cubs. The cubs had been walking exactly in the tracks of their mother, and because their own tracks were slightly smaller, had not completely covered the adult female's tracks. This example carried the concept of "perfect walking" to a higher level.

It would be interesting to speculate on the adaptive significance of such a unified single-file procession. Three cats would make far less noise if they were nearing prey, but there are no known examples of cougars—even family units—hunting together. How they could walk so perfectly is as astounding as why they would. Power has seen it more

In the final rush, cougars travel nearly forty miles
per hour in twenty-foot bounds.

In rocky country, the trail of a cougar is invisible.

than once, but only smiles and shrugs when the how and why questions are asked.

The "stride" of a cougar, or the distance between tracks parallel to the cat's direction of travel, ranges between one-and-a-half and three feet. Slow travel by a small cougar represents the lower end of this range and a big cat in a hurry takes the longest strides. From side to side, the "straddle" distance between tracks is a foot or less. Most dog family members have a comparatively narrow straddle distance, probably to enhance straight-ahead speed. For a stalker like the cougar, the balance advantage of a wide stance would enable the cat to freeze in almost any position. Since a cougar moves slower than wolves and coyotes most of the time, the tracks of a cougar usually have more detail.

Once, while cross-country skiing in Northern Montana, I followed the tracks of three cougars. One track was large, about five inches across, and the other two were about four inches across. The impressions were fairly well defined, but the snow was melting that day, and I guessed that the tracks had probably enlarged themselves a half-inch by melting out. The larger cougar was moving more directly than the other two, almost in a straight line. The other two were taking side trips every fifty feet, investigating creek bottoms, a culvert, side trails and the tracks of a red squirrel. From what I know of adolescent behavior, this was not an unusual pattern of behavior. I could almost picture the mother cougar rolling her eyes at the wasted energy and antics of the nearly-grown cubs. She was providing for three, no doubt, and was all business.

I have seen cougar tail "tracks" in deep snow. This particular cougar was bounding, causing its tail to bounce and make an impression. The impression was slight, even in two-and-a-half feet of soft snow, so I suspect that cougar tails are carried high most of the time, and that I was looking at a rare phenomenon. It was helpful in this case, however. I was in northern Minnesota, a state without a resident cougar population, and had seen the cougar bound across the road in front of my car. Until I saw the tail impressions, I wasn't completely believing my eyes.

Scat

Cougar scat is usually about an inch in diameter and consists of different-length segments with deep constrictions between them. By contrast, canids and some weasel family members drop scat which tapers to pointed ends—the ends usually made of hair from the prey animal.

Identifying cougar scat is easier than it first appears, but not because of the shape of the scat itself. The forest floor is always in good supply of "cat litter." A feline is a feline, and just like domestic cousins, cougars almost always cover their scat with debris. The dog family and other predators like wolverines and fishers are less fastidious.

It has been said by old trackers that the scratchings of a cougar covering scat are on the side of the dung heap that corresponds to the direction the cat was traveling. I would amend that by saying it is probably on the side where the cat *intended* to travel. Nothing precludes a cougar from changing its mind.

Caches

The cougar habit of burying scat is not the only expression of this behavior. They also "cache" their kills, burying them before they leave from the first feeding. Often the debris cougars use to bury the kill is hair from the animal killed. They pluck, and sometimes shear, hair from the dead animal with their teeth and claws before feeding, which also relates to the shape of cougar scat. With very little hair passing through their digestive system, they don't have the raw material for the tapered ends typical of canine scat.

The urge to bury the carcass is so strong in cougars that there have been times when, on bare hard ground, a single twig "covers" the dead animal. Depending on weather and the size of the prey, a cougar may come back to feed on the dead animal up to a dozen times. They usually move the carcass after each feeding by dragging it to another cache spot, which is often a hundred yards from the first.

Cache sites are usually under trees with low branches, if there are trees in the vicinity. Drag marks usually point the way to the cache site. Moving a kill under a tree probably increases the time before magpies and ravens discover the free food, and advertise it to other watchful

Above: Cougars have a preference for deer, but like most predators, are opportunistic.

Following pages: Despite the caching habits of cougars, competition is rarely far away.

Young cougars start with small prey and work their way up.

scavengers. Hiding the kill only delays the inevitable, because scavenging birds have very sharp vision. In fact, one of the best ways to see a cougar is to watch for concentrations of magpie, raven and eagle activity, and set up a stakeout. Experienced cougar watchers and photographers don't really watch for cougars. They watch first the birds, which will inevitably lead them to the cougar cache site.

The kill itself is usually a good cougar sign. Of all the large predators, cougars are easily the most efficient at killing. Most of the time, a single bite to the back of the neck separates the vertebrae and the spinal cord in a microsecond. Less experienced cougars sometimes need a second bite on the windpipe. The same is true of ten-year-old or older cougars, whose brittle teeth break off easily, making the killing bite impossible. Either way, the prey is still killed relatively quickly.

Cougar mouths are wider than coyote or wolf mouths, and the marks of the "eye teeth," or (ironically) the canine teeth, on the neck of the prey are about two inches apart on a cougar kill. There are also scratch marks on the back and sides of the prey animal. Cougars which have been digging quite a lot (looking for ground squirrels) will wear down their claws, causing a vicious cycle which may eventually lead to their death. If the cat cannot hold a deer or elk firmly, with sharp claws, they are often thrown from the back of the prey, and cannot administer the coup de grace. If they get hungry, they may go back to digging for more small prey, compounding the initial problem.

Cougars usually pluck hair before beginning to feed, and the first meal is usually the heart, lungs and liver, which are removed from just behind the rib cage. These entrails are a cougar's sole source of valuable vitamin A.

After that, according to cougar etiquette, the underside of the hams is usually course number two. Cougar researchers have seen exceptions to this "normal" pattern. At one time or other, the first feeding on a cougar kill has been some other part, almost as if there was some kind of craving for a certain "cut," like the rib-eye. The weirdest example I have heard of came from Gary Power, who described a carcass which had most of the bones missing, and the meat still intact. Calcium deficiency, perhaps?

If the entire prey is eaten, even the bones, chances are better that the kill was made by a female with cubs. Sometimes a solitary adult will abandon part of a prey animal, for a variety of reasons. It may be simple wanderlust and nervous energy which makes them travel on; it could be the availability of other prey. One thing is certain, however, and that is returning to the same spot day after day becomes increasingly dangerous to a cougar, especially when human predators are around.

Scenting

Solitary animals are faced with a problem when it is mating time. How do they find each other efficiently? The cougar's senses are acute, but they have large home ranges, and encountering another cougar by chance alone would probably be too inefficient for the species.

Mature males often scrape dirt or debris into a mound with either their forepaws or hind feet. Sometimes, but not always, they may urinate or defecate on top of the mound (unlike ordinary covered scat piles). There is some conjecture among cougar scientists that the scrapes either serve some loose territorial function between males or they advertise the presence of a male to females, or both.

The scrapes seem to be more abundant where the home ranges of two or more cougars overlap. Scrapes could function as a way to make mating more efficient, but it is difficult to interpret motivation in the actions of another animal. They could be scraping for no apparent reason.

Dens

Male cougars don't use dens, and females only use them for birthing and raising cubs. The "den" of a cougar female is rarely the classic cave seen in the movies. The base of a thick tree or the area under a windfall or horizontal ledge is a more likely place for a female to give birth and raise a litter of cubs.

In Idaho, for instance, there are no shortages of crevices, openings in large rock piles and even old mine shafts—all of which are used by cougars. Obviously, the area will look trampled farther and farther away from the birth site as the cubs grow and explore their surroundings.

There is no special "preparation" of a den by the female, other than some minor excavation in some cases. No material is brought in

Cougar mothers leave the den area only to hunt.

for bedding. They simply occupy whatever cavity is available, without modifications.

Some females take more of a "mobile home" approach to denning. Once, a female cougar with two young cubs made a kill about seven air miles (over very steep, rugged country) from the den. The kill was made just at dusk. By the next morning she had both cubs at the kill site, teaching them to eat solid food. This cougar continued to move her cubs to the kill each time she made a new one.

Sightings

Of course, the best sign of a cougar is a cougar. If you ever see one in the wild, you can be sure of two things—you are lucky indeed, and your heartbeat is faster than it was a moment ago.

If an observer is patient and persistent, isolated cougar signs can be transformed into stories. It is not always the signs themselves which tell the story. For instance, one researcher, over a period of weeks, was noticing that a cougar was staying in creek and river bottoms, eating porcupines, beavers and other small game. From the choice of habitat and the cougar's behavior, he was able to piece together that the cougar was old, probably infirm somehow, and unable to kill larger game on the slopes above. Later, he captured that same cougar and examined its four broken canines. But the satisfaction came from already knowing what he would find.

Once a cougar sign is found, the good detective pieces all the early evidence into possible scenarios, gradually narrowing them into a single story line in which there are no inconsistencies. The reading of these stories gives us clues to the mystery called "cougar."

Above: Cubs spend their first weeks of life in or near the den.

Following pages: A mother may move the cubs to new den sites as often as every few days.

Vital Statistics

About fifty million years ago cats and dogs split from a common ancestor. The first felines were very much like saber-toothed cats. Since that time, the cats have branched many times, and many taxonomists have been gainfully employed trying to map what happened through the years. Lately, genetic mapping has shed some light on the evolution of cats. It appears as though ocelots split from the family tree first. The ancestors of domestic cats branched from the main group around nine million years ago and the cougar split about four or five million years ago. The genetic story has had some surprising twists. For instance, there was, until ten thousand years ago, a cat almost identical to a cheetah in North America, but it was a close relative of the cougar, and genetically very different from the African cheetah. Also, lynxes and bobcats, it seems, are relatives of lions and tigers, but are very different from the cougar.

Taxonomists will continue to argue and refine, no doubt, but the bottom line is that modern cougars have been around for about three million years. Twenty-six separate subspecies of cougar are recognized by some taxonomists, but they all interbreed and would be generally recognized as a large, tawny, small-headed, long-tailed cougar. It is important to understand the versatility of this animal. The twenty-six subspecies of cougars are found (or were, in some cases) in the Rocky

Uncomfortable in open spaces, cougars are
always on the lookout.

Mountains, Eastern big woods, the great prairies, Central and South American rain forests, and the Andes and pampas of Argentina. If prey animals were not so scarce in the Arctic, they would probably live there, too.

Fur

The cougar's scientific name, *Felis concolor*, literally means "cat of one color." Although cougar cubs have spots until they are about six months old, the cougar's single color, along with a proportionally small head and long tail, make it easily recognizable. The spots on a young cougar fade slowly, and are actually visible at close range until they are almost two years old. The color of mature cougars ranges from gold to gray to reddish, but the cheeks and outer ears are always darker, and the "mustache," chin and lower chest are creamy white. Adults molt every year, but not much is known about the differences between summer and winter fur of cougars. The long, thick tail of the cougar is tipped with darker color.

Experienced cougar scientists can usually distinguish at first glance between adult males and females, and they can spot a young cougar quickly. Males are not only larger, but they have a more massive neck and rounder face and ears. Females tend to have a thinner, more angular face and pointed ears. One researcher was fooled by a female which had frostbitten ears, and the tips had rounded off.

Young cougars have a "teddy bear look," according to Gary Power, and have a very fluffy tail, much thicker than an adult's. Transient young cougars (without an established home hunting area) are almost always thinner, reflecting their unrefined hunting skills and lack of suitable ambush spots.

Most species of mammals have a black (melanistic) phase, like the black panther, which is really a different-colored variety of the African leopard. Most also have an albino variation. There are no records of either variation in North America, and they are extremely rare in South America. It is difficult to generalize on the reasons behind this uniformity, but a good guess would be a smaller amount of genetic variation in the cougar gene pool. I can only imagine how difficult it would be for a white cougar to stalk enough deer to reach breeding age.

Above: When their claws are retracted, cougar paws give little hint of the armament they contain.

Following pages: Like all cats, the cougar brain has a large area devoted to balance and coordination.

males are over eight feet in total length. Certainly they have the size and power to take down a mature elk—and stimulate the thoughts of a two-legged hiker.

Female cougars have eight nipples (six are functional), and the condition of those nipples can tell much about the life and history of that female. Young transient females have small, white nipples. A female which has nursed young has larger, distended, dark nipples. Since females don't usually breed until they have an established home range, this condition is also a good indicator of a "resident" female. Females which are presently or recently nursing also have blackened areas of hair around the nipples. This condition can be seen at a long distance, an obvious advantage to the observing researcher.

No members of the cat family can convert vitamin B-carotene into vitamin A, like many other mammals can. That means that the liver, lungs, and kidneys of prey are its only good source of vitamin A, and therefore are what cougars usually eat first after a kill. Most healthy cougars eat an average of four to eight pounds of meat per day, but again that's an average between no food on many days and gorging on other days.

Wild animals don't die strictly of old age, so the twenty-one years one cougar lived in captivity is not indicative of life span. The only requirement for longevity in the wild is that some animals live long enough to reproduce. In general, cougars die in hundreds of ways at all ages. An average life span, given these variables, is around fifteen years.

Claws

Cougars have retractile-protractile claws, which function mainly for holding prey while the killing bite is administered. The claws are extended automatically by a hinge system in the bones and tendons. A cougar cannot "reach" with its front paw without exposing its claws.

A claw on a healthy cougar is about an inch and a half long. The claws are not razor sharp—but close to it. Cougars with broken teeth usually have to dig for small game, so their claws are usually worn down to dull nubs.

Cougars can climb almost as fast as they can run.

The gape and spacing of canine teeth
are ideal for breaking the necks of deer.

Jaws

The bite of a cougar is very powerful. The sagittal crest, a large bone ridge down the center of the skull, connects to massive temporal muscles, which in turn connect to the inside of the jaw. Another muscle, the masseter (or masticating muscle) connects the upper and lower jaws directly on the outside. Those huge jaw muscles attach quite far forward on the short jaw and skull, giving the mouth a mechanical advantage, which translates to about a ton of pressure per square inch. Calling a cougar bite "vise-like" is an understatement.

Teeth

Adult cougars have twenty-four teeth; twelve on the top and twelve on the bottom. The bite itself is done with the canine teeth; the carnassial teeth farther back in the mouth are slicing teeth, for tearing meat and chopping bones into swallowing size.

Very little actual chewing is done by carnivores because they lack the back teeth needed for grinding; it is also probably in their best interest to eat quickly and leave to avoid danger. The gulping of large chunks of meat means that the digestive tract of cougars must do most of the work. Like most carnivores, the digestive acids and enzymes are very potent in cougars.

The canine teeth are spaced just perfectly to penetrate on both sides of deer neck vertebrae, further evidence that the deer and cougar have evolved together as a perfectly matched "set" of predator and prey.

At about six to eight months of age, a cougar's permanent canine teeth come in next to the deciduous canines. For a while, there are eight canine teeth in a young cougar's jaw.

The importance of a cougar's prime weapon, its canines, is illustrated by another Gary Power story. He treed and drugged a young male that was thin, weighing sixty-seven pounds. It had broken one of its canines, and the stub of broken tooth was swollen and abscessed. It was obviously very painful for this animal to apply a killing bite, and its low body weight reflected that difficulty. Power temporarily pushed his objective detachment aside and did a little surgery. With his knife, he gouged out the abscessed tooth and applied some camphor to help it heal. Later, the cougar woke from the muscle relaxant and left. As luck would have it, Power was able to recapture the same cougar a year later. It weighed 155 pounds and looked very healthy.

Noses

Cougars also have vibrissae, the whiskers familiar in most felines. In many animals, vibrissae serve as a width gauge. They are usually about as wide as the animal is wide, so, before an irreversible commitment is made to enter a hole or squeeze between two trees, the vibrissae instantly tell whether it is possible. Cougar whiskers are thought to function in the same way. Some biologists speculate that the vibrissae assist in the instantaneous decision about where to apply the killing bite on prey. It is like an automatic "trigger" effect: when the whiskers touch neck muscle, the jaws snap shut. The entire area of cougar mouths and teeth are connected to more nerves and therefore are more sensitive than in most mammals. Again, this could be helpful in applying the crucial bite.

Cougar noses are probably not as important for locating prey as they would be for wolves and coyotes. The logical reason for concluding this would be the relative size of the inner nasal surface. After all, wolves have eight times the olfactory surface area in their noses as a cougar does. Diane Ackerman, in her book *A Natural History of the Senses*, relates that the nasal surface area doesn't correspond to the number of cells. Humans have 50 million olafactory (smelling) cells and wolves have 200 million. Cougars are somewhere in between.

The real reason wolves have a much better sense of smell is that a much larger part of the brain is set aside for interpreting smells. In cougars, the size of that area is about half the size of a wolf's. In humans, it is tiny by comparison. The real reason we cannot smell as well as most mammals is we are not "smart" enough.

Vocalizations

The cat family, or Felidae, has two genera: those that roar (lions, tigers, leopards, jaguars) in *Panthera*; and those that don't, in *Felis*.

Potential prey or potential danger demands the undivided attention of a cougar.

While not as sensitive as wolf or coyote noses, cougar noses are used for many hunting and communication functions.

Animals in this second genus, which includes domestic cats and the cougar, don't have the proper resonating chamber in their throats for the roar, but they do make many sounds.

Cougars don't exactly "meow," but they don't roar either. Imagine the sounds made by your house cats, then lower the pitch and increase the volume (pretend your cat weighs two hundred pounds); this is the range of sounds made by a cougar. They purr, they yowl, and they "caterwaul"—the loud, incessant yowling made by mating cats. Some native peoples thought that the caterwauling was a sign of death. Perhaps it was, but the cats were just doing their version of a romantic duet.

The "growl" of the cougar, made with ears back and hair raised, is a defensive threat that means "leave me alone!" Actually, it is a rather feeble sounding threat, because it has very little volume and reso- nance and is fairly high-pitched compared to the roaring cats.

The range of vocalizations in cougars is limited compared to more social animals, like wolves. Since cougars practice mutual avoid- ance, other than when mating, they have little need for many different kinds of vocal communication.

One exception, however, is a high-pitched "chirp," which most lis- teners would interpret as a bird call. Its purpose is one type of com- munication between mothers and cubs.

Scents

The world of scent communication is a mystery to us, so we must guess when we say that cougars probably use their eyes and ears much more than their noses for locating prey. It appears that the nose comes into play more for mating and territorial purposes. When investigating the scrapes of another male cougar, or a urine spot of a female, males curl their lips and nose into a grimace called a "flehmen" posture. This posture is done by many mammals, including deer and elk, during the mating season.

Biologists speculate that the flehmen exposes a more sensitive olfactory area in the nasal passage. It's much like cranking up the power in a microscope by flipping to a more powerful lens. It may play a role in determining whether a cougar female is in heat. For scent expression, besides the normal excretory functions, cougars have anal glands, glands near the mouth and ears, and (possibly) interdigital glands between the toes. All of the above have functions completely unknown to us.

Eyes and Ears

A sight-feeder would be expected to have good vision. Cougar eyes are large and yellow, with large pupils for nocturnal (night) and crepuscular (dawn and dusk) light gathering. Some cats have pupils which contract into slits, enabling them to open the pupil wider than those animals with round pupils. These animals have habits which are almost completely nocturnal. Cougar pupils are round, leading to the logical conclusion that they have a bit more day-night versatility in their hunting habits.

The retina (movie screen) in a cougar's eye has two features which enable better night vision. First, there are far more "rod" cells in the retina than "cone" cells. Cone cells are color-sensitive, and rod cells see light intensity, or brightness. Cone cells need high light intensity to work properly and are dominant in diurnal (daytime) animals, such as humans, most birds and squirrels. Rod cells are extremely sensitive in low light conditions.

The second feature of the cougar retina which helps night vision is a reflective layer behind the rods and cones which prevents light from being absorbed and lost. When headlights pick up the "glowing" eyes of a deer or cougar, it is this reflective layer which is seen by the passengers and, hopefully, the driver.

Cougar eyes are located on the front of the head, as they are in most predators. This configuration allows for binocular vision. Using some instinctive trigonometry, the brain can accurately estimate distance with the two-eyed approach—which would be critical for a stalking animal. By contrast, most prey animals have eyes on the sides of their heads. Their visual field is nearly 360 degrees, so they can see danger coming from all directions. If it is danger, it doesn't matter much exactly how far away it is—what matters is that it is seen at all.

Occasionally, scientists trap and tag a cougar which has lost an eye. Although the loss of an eye doesn't always mean a quick death for

Above: Females lead a busy life when hunting for three or four.

Following pages: A cougar is the epitome of physical efficiency—all muscle and bone.

Status
and Distribution

Part of the reason cougars have so many names is that they cover such a huge range. Two hundred years ago, the cougar ranged from the tree line in Canada to the southern tip of South America. They were in what is now forty-nine states, all the provinces, and ranged over every inch of Central and South America, from sea level to almost 15,000 feet. They had no trouble adapting to every climate and terrain on two continents. "Versatility" is certainly a descriptive understatement.

Although cougar numbers are certainly down from two hundred years ago, they still range over all of Central and South America. The big change is really in the eastern United States and Canada. They now range across only two of the eleven provinces, Alberta and British Columbia, and the thirteen westernmost states. A tiny population, somewhere between thirty and fifty animals, holds on in the Florida Everglades. If human population were plotted against cougar population on a map of North America, the densities of each would be perfect opposites, with absolutely no coincidence. Cougars are where people aren't.

The subspecies of cougars have been deduced through sophisticated cranial and teeth measurements, relative sizes, color patterns and quirky things such as the kink in the end of a Florida panther's tail. (Eastern cougars are commonly referred to as "panthers" but they are the same

Cougars have adapted to every forested area
in the Western Hemisphere.

species.) Most people would not be able to instantly recognize the difference between *Felis concolor hippolestes* from Wyoming, Colorado, Nebraska and the Dakotas, and *Felis concolor missoulensis* from Idaho, Montana and Alberta. Also, there are no strict boundaries between the subspecies. They freely interbreed and usually show characteristics of each kind where their ranges overlap. Subspecies simply represent geographical variation—*slight* variation.

In most cases, the differences between subspecies of cougars would be academic, in both the literal and figurative sense. Today, there is some interest in subspecies differences because of interest in reintroduction programs for species which have been eradicated from their former ranges. For instance, if there was a remnant population of *Felis concolor couguar*, the Eastern panther, in Nova Scotia, and there was enough interest and support in Northern Maine to reintroduce cougars there by transplantation, it would make sense to find the cougars with genetics as closely resembling the original population as possible—namely, the same subspecies from Nova Scotia. The reasoning behind this: varieties of animals which evolved in the Northeast would be better adapted to the climate and conditions of the Northeast, and have a better chance of survival. Perhaps the fur of a cougar from the Northeast is more waterproof and thicker than the fur from a cougar in Arizona.

The example just given is probably "academic" in one sense of the word. Most scientists believe that the Eastern panther is extinct. There have been sightings of cougars from Quebec to South Carolina, but they are rarely considered "reliable" sightings. The possibility that the observed cougars are escapees from game farms, or are transient young cougars that are known to range hundreds of miles before they settle into a home area, injects quite a bit of skepticism into the idea of a resident population.

Not everyone is convinced that the Eastern panther is gone, however. If ever there was a difficult animal to see, it is the cougar. It is elusive and nocturnal. It consistently avoids human population. And the sightings, especially along the Appalachian Crest, persist. There have always been more cougars around than it seems, and those who believe that *F. c. couguar* is still viable take some satisfaction in knowing that. The human need to hope is an unmeasurable part of the

Above: Yellow eyes, pink nose, white muzzle—typical cougar facial coloration.

Following pages: The ability to "freeze" anytime during a stalk is critical.

equation. That tendency confounds statisticians, but it plays a huge role in defining the human condition. Despite our feeble attempts at controlling our surroundings, we want mystery in our lives, we want to be the one to see the cougar where it should not be.

Thirty subspecies of cougar have been categorized, thirteen in North America, two in Central America and fifteen in South America. Most of us would not be able to tell one variety from another, especially in adjacent subspecies which interbreed. The visual differences are slight. There is some variance across the entire range of cougars which is clearer to the average observer. The color of cougars is more reddish in tropical subspecies. In the desert subspecies, they are light tan. In the mountains and forests they are grayer and darker. The color differences make perfect sense if camouflage has any survival value, which it surely does.

The average size of cougars is larger in the far North and at the southern tip of South America, and smaller near the Equator. These differences are consistent with a principle in biology which has to do with the conservation of heat by most species. Bergmann's Rule states that races from cooler climates tend to be larger than races of the same species living in warmer climates. Being larger in cooler places would be an advantage because a larger animal has more volume (a larger furnace) for heat production. As an animal grows, its surface area (radiator, for losing heat to the atmosphere) does not grow in proportion to its volume. The ratio between the furnace and radiator size becomes larger—in other words, the animal can produce more heat and lose it at a slower rate. In colder climates, the advantage of producing more heat and losing it slower is fairly obvious. In the tropics, the reverse is true. Being smaller, with a relatively larger surface area, enables an animal to get rid of excess heat. The balance between heat produced and heat lost determines the temperature of an animal at any given time, and the thermal efficiency of an animal over the long run, so nature has selected for smaller cougars in the tropics and larger ones in the far north and south.

Besides the *couguar*, *missoulensis* and *hippolestes* subspecies, there are (or at least were) ten more in North America. *Felis concolor californica* resides primarily in California; *F. c. oregonensis* lives in the Pacific Northwest; *F. c. vancouverensis* is a relatively more aggressive cougar

The tawny color of a cougar blends well into many backgrounds.

Females may take maturing cubs on a hunt, but only one at a time.

from Vancouver Island; *F. c. browni* inhabits a smaller area, the lower Colorado River Basin; and *F. c. improcera* lives only on the Baja Peninsula of Mexico. In Arizona, New Mexico and south far into Mexico, the light-colored *F. c. azteca* is the resident cougar. *F. c. kaibabensis* lives in the Basin and Range deserts of the Kaibab Plateau, Nevada, Utah and Southeast Oregon.

Farther east, *F. c. schorgeri* once inhabited the midwestern states and Southern Ontario, although it is rarely sighted and is possibly extinct. Texas, Oklahoma, Arkansas and eastern New Mexico are the homes of *F. c. stanleyana*.

Felis concolor coryi once inhabited the entire Southeast from Louisiana to South Carolina, but the only area where it now can be found is extreme South Florida. This subspecies is truly a "swamp cat," living exclusively in the Everglades (the "cataglade" would be a good colloquialism to counterpoint the "catamount" from the Northeast). About thirty to fifty Florida panthers are alive today, and the population is probably very inbred and on its way to extinction. Some of the identifying characteristics of the *coryi* subspecies, such as the kinked tail, a cowlick on the back hair, and failure of one of the male's testicles to descend, may actually be signs of an inbred population. It is listed as an endangered subspecies by the U.S. Fish and Wildlife Service, and is probably the most endangered large mammal in the Western Hemisphere.

South of the border, the status of cougars is mostly unknown. Logic would suggest that a similar shrinking of range has happened in Central and South America, and it is probably the least human-inhabited areas which have the most cougars. A good guess would be that sizable populations exist in the Andes, Patagonia, and the rain forests which have yet to be slashed and burned.

In general, *Felis concolor* as a species is certainly not endangered. In some areas of the Rocky Mountains, their populations are actually growing. But if we look at separate populations of cougars as genetically adapted to their ranges, then the story is different. The gene pool, or the amount of variability, in any species is like an insurance policy against extinction. If a new disease nearly wiped out the entire population of *F. c. missoulensis*, but *F. c. kaibabensis* was resistant, it would certainly be an advantage to have a population of *kaibabensis* around.

The relationship between roadless areas and surrounding areas with easier access reveals much about the "micro-distribution" of cougars. Researchers in the Idaho Primitive Area, a large roadless place composed of the adjacent River of No Return and Selway-Bitterroot Wilderness areas, have documented the differences between a disturbed and undisturbed population of cougars. Several researchers independently noted that in the roadless area, over ninety percent of the population were resident cougars. The remaining fraction was almost all juveniles, and there were almost no adolescent, transient cougars. This tightly organized population contrasted sharply with the surrounding areas, which had around fifty percent established, settled residents. The other half of the population was equally divided between transients and juveniles.

The greater cougar hunting pressure was, the greater the number of juveniles in subsequent years. There are a number of speculations which can be made about this relationship between the two populations. The reproductive rate (or at least the survival rate of juveniles) is low when cougars are allowed to exist without human-caused mortality. The cougars in a heavily hunted population have more cubs (or their survival rate is higher) in order to keep pace with the number of deer and elk.

This also suggests that these stable wilderness areas are "seed" places for the whole population. Many of the transient cougars in surrounding areas are dispersing from the "occupied" country, where there is little room for new residents (because the residents there live to ripe old ages). In fact, the Central Idaho roadless area is a "feeder" system for Western Montana and the remainder of Idaho.

Whatever the source of mortality, when it increases, cougar population distributions adjust. Increased mortality invariably raises the number of transient cougars and decreases the number of residents, in proportion to the amount of mortality. This relationship has some practical applications. Without knowing the actual population of cougars, a wildlife manager can still use ratios between adolescent and adult cougars to guard against over-hunting and protect a viable population.

Knowing any species' status and distribution has obvious advantages in the "management" of that species. But in the case of the cougar, there is another advantage which is obvious, but we humans don't like to acknowledge. Because cougars are where humans aren't, the distribution of the cougar can be thought of as a general indicator of the health of the land.

*Above: Cougars almost never "drop" onto prey from above, but they often climb
to higher elevations to spot potential prey.*

Following pages: The Florida panther subspecies often has flecks of white on its head and back.

Cougar Habits

We know less about the cougar than about any other large animal in North America. The reasons—shy, elusive, solitary, nocturnal—are obvious, and already mentioned in this book. The redundancy is for emphasis. There are only inadequate superlatives for how elusive this animal is.

I have spent years of my life in the woods. I've lived in remote places most of the time I have been alive. I've seen wild wolves at least a dozen times, black bears maybe fifty, grizzlies seven or eight times, and cougars exactly twice.

Fortunately for would-be cougar writers, there are people who have forced the issue with cougars. They have treed them with trained dogs and radio-collared them, tracked them from helicopters, combed their home ranges for sign of any kind, and pieced together a fuzzy picture of everyday cougar life.

The easiest things to deduce from radio-tracking are the "where" questions. Where do cougars spend most of their time? What do they call "home"? Of course, the answer is different for every area of the Western Hemisphere. A Florida panther's home is wet, thick and flat. A western cougar's is dry, steep and rocky. A Vancouver Island cougar's is wet, thick, steep and rocky. We could get specific and say, for instance, that the Central Idaho cougar prefers dense, but not too dense, Douglas

The cougar's acute senses, solitary ways, and its preference
for wilderness have kept it mysterious to humans.

Young transient cougars eat whatever they can catch.

fir and ponderosa pine stands mixed with small sage and grass openings. This description of cougar habitat also describes nearly all of central Idaho. The cougar doesn't like large openings in the timber, but will freely cross them at night to access other hunting areas. Logic would say that stalking would be nearly impossible in open areas, but surprisingly few large sage and mountain mahogany bushes are required for stalking cover.

Food

All thirty subspecies of cougars would have their own habitat descriptions, but the portraits would just describe the dominant cover of their areas. Cougars don't decide where to live, anyway. That job belongs to deer. Cougars are where the deer are, and where the humans aren't. The only exceptions to that rule are in Chile and Peru, where there are no deer, but good substitutes, like guanacos, agoutis and pacas.

As their tooth structure might suggest, cougars are totally carnivorous. On the rare occasion when vegetable matter has been found in a cougar gut, it has probably been eaten by accident. Deer are the usual preference, and when deer are not available for some reason, cougars consistently choose the next largest prey animal they can find. In Florida, that animal is a wild hog. In the West, it is a bighorn sheep or an elk. They also eat raccoons, beavers, hares, porcupines and wild horses opportunistically. Sometimes Columbia ground squirrels help a Rocky Mountain cougar through the summer. But the meal of choice is venison. Every behavior and adaptation of the cougar seems aimed at deer—whitetails in the East and mule deer in the West. It is probably no evolutionary coincidence that the cougar's canine teeth are spaced exactly right to penetrate on both sides of a deer neck vertebrae, or that the reach of front paws hugs a deer's shoulders just far enough down to make escape unlikely.

Since it is really deer that choose the general habitat of cougars, we can get specific only about cover types. Cougars need enough cover to stalk about fifty feet from the prey, but not so much cover that they make noise during the stalk. The final rush and pounce would be too noisy in very thick cover, and a straight-line opening to the prey would be an advantage. Deer, on the other hand, can bound over and zig-zag through extremely thick cover much more effectively than a cougar. In general, lots of trees and little undergrowth are to the cougar's advantage, and thick undergrowth translates to escape for a deer.

Some peripheral evidence supports this idea. Cougar kill sites are "clumped" in certain areas, suggesting that it is easier to stalk effectively in those places. Most of the clumped kill sites are in moderately (not extremely) thick cover.

An average-sized cougar needs about ten pounds of meat per day. Extrapolating, that translates to around thirty deer each year. The number of deer killed by cougars actually ranges from ten to ninety deer each year, or about one every four to fourteen days. The wide range in these numbers has more to do with the countryside than the appetite of cougars. A part of the disparity can be explained, for example, by a big male eating twice as much as a transient yearling, but that can't account for one cougar killing eight times as many as another. Perhaps one cougar is routinely chased from kills by bears, wolves or humans, and another rarely encounters any competition. Another explanation, at least in the Southwest, is that a desert cat has to deal with heat and spoilage. In the desert heat, after three to four days the kill is rotten, so a cougar is forced to make another kill.

When deer populations are abundant and stalking is relatively easy, a cougar may leave one kill to make another sooner than in years of scarcity. And, perhaps, the different killing rates can be chalked up to something as simple as variety. It may seem wasteful to us when a cougar kills often. Rest assured, however, that "waste" is not in the conceptual framework of the cougar or of nature itself. Any deer or elk carcass abandoned by a cougar becomes a virtual ecosystem of scavengers and decomposers, which depend on the cougar being somewhat "wasteful."

A female with cubs has to kill for four, in some cases. To be more efficient, females with young concentrate more on larger prey, only rarely killing a hare, raccoon or beaver. A study in Utah showed that the average days between kills for a solitary female was sixteen days, for a female with three-month-old cubs it was nine days, and for a female with fifteen-month-old cubs it was three days.

Cougar and deer—an evolutionary partnership.

Range

Cougars are loners, for the most part. The area one cougar uses is called its "home range." The home range of male cougars varies from only twenty-five square miles to over five hundred square miles. For females, home ranges are smaller; anywhere between ten and four hundred square miles. The size of an individual's home range probably reflects the accessibility of adequate prey—in other words, there could be just as many deer in a twenty-five-square-mile area of southern Florida as there is in a five hundred-square-mile area of southern Utah or Nevada. The Basin and Range area of Utah, Nevada and Eastern Oregon has isolated mountain ranges with vast playa deserts between them. There, the range of a cougar must be huge just to find deer. The actual area of hunting use, however, is probably much smaller. Deer are mostly found in the "range" part of the basin and range country. The cougar may have to travel between two or three small ranges to find enough prey. The stark playas between those ranges are part of a cougar home area, but are used for travel only.

The home ranges of female cougars often overlap some, but never completely. Male home ranges seldom overlap other males', but overlap several female ranges. When a home range is defended, it becomes a "territory" as well. The non-overlap of male home ranges suggests some territoriality among males. The fact that males also make most of the scrapes further suggests that they may be important in territorial marking. Not much is known about cougar territoriality, if it exists, but it is clear that (except for mating) there is a mutual avoidance which is practiced by the xenophobic cat.

The choice of home range is probably a matter of chance. When a yearling cougar leaves its mother, it wanders until it can hunt an area without encountering other cougars very often. If the "transient" is a male, and it encounters another "resident" male, it often gets chased off or even killed. Many animals have a strong affinity to their home ranges, and when they are captured and relocated, will sometimes travel thousands of miles to return to their former range. Not so with cougars. The cougars which are relocated seem the settle into the new area, which is more evidence that the location of an individual cougar's home range is a matter of fate.

Above: A Florida panther's home range is as much water as dry land.

Following pages: Adult cougars do not have the bushy-tailed "teddy bear" look of young transients.

Transient males don't scrape until they have settled into a home range, which suggests that even among cougars, some discretion is the better part of valor. Because a transient is inexperienced and wanders until it doesn't encounter other cougars and can settle-in, transients are often more desperate for food, and are more often the victims of human predation.

Adult male cougars sometimes kill transients which show up in the adult's home range. Females whose ranges overlap a male's range must be especially vigilant when they have cubs. There are many reports of cannibalism by males on unattended cubs—a cougar male seems to have no genetic restraints on modifying this behavior. It is perhaps a downside of solitary lifestyles.

Activity

Home ranges may differ seasonally, especially in the mountain West. In my home state of Idaho, there is a seasonal migration of elk and deer vertically (as much as four or five thousand feet) and horizontally (as much as fifty miles). Some cougars are lucky enough to have both summer and winter prey ranges within their home range. If they don't, they adjust. In some cases the spring/summer/fall home range of a cougar is completely different than its winter range—by necessity.

Within their Northern Rocky Mountain home ranges, cougars typically move about ten miles per day. A normal activity pattern would be one hour of movement followed by a half-hour of rest, repeated throughout the dusk, night and dawn parts of the day. During daylight hours they are less active. When a cougar is said to be nocturnal and/or crepuscular, it means they are somewhat more active during those hours. The terms are relative, at least for cougars.

Some animals, like foxes, have regular cyclic travel routes. Cougar movement is more random within their home range. Again, if territory were very important to male cougars, we would expect to see some "patrolling" of the home range edge, and see more scrapes along those edges. We don't. Scraping is done nearly anywhere within the home range.

When cougars are moving between hunting areas, they tend to travel in relatively straight lines. When they are in "hunt mode," the travel

A typical activity pattern for a cougar is "move an hour, rest a half-hour."

path is much slower and erratic, zigging and zagging to locate prey.

The hunting cougar's body posture is a low crouch, and it almost "slinks" from one hidden observation point to another. Once prey is spotted, a cougar operates with a single-minded intensity. Staying in the low crouch, it moves forward in spurts, seldom taking its unwavering stare from the prey. The cougar's neck is stretched far forward in a state of fierce alertness. When the prey animal is looking its way, it freezes in place. Sometimes the cougar's excitement level is betrayed by an involuntary twitching of the end of its tail, but that movement is shielded from the prey's eyes by the cougar's body. If possible, cougars will stalk from above and behind the prey, to within fifty feet or less.

Cougars regularly kill bull elk, and sometimes kill even larger prey such as mature moose. In those cases, the cougar's mouth is simply not large enough to apply a killing bite. Gary Power has noticed claw marks on the noses of cougar-killed mature bull elk and mules, and the marks could be there for two different reasons: One, cougars often drag larger prey to a cache site by their noses. But he also speculates that the killing technique on large animals is different from that on deer. It is possible that when a cougar surprises a mature bull elk, it grabs the far shoulder and the nose with its claws. It pulls back hard on the nose, "bulldogging" the moose into a hard fall, which breaks its neck. It is an interesting variation on the preferred killing technique of the cougar—the separating of neck vertebrae. Until someone sees it happen, it will have to remain speculation.

A cougar's teeth are extremely sensitive to touch, allowing an instantaneous adjustment in the location of the killing bite. The cougar hunting technique is best characterized by an almost surgical "precision." In fact, it has been speculated that a cougar could have a kill success rate as high as eighty percent. But many researchers feel that the average success rate is probably closer to fifty percent. In wolf packs, the hunting philosophy is different. Potential prey is "tested" with a few false rushes, and the slowest one becomes the victim. Perhaps it is not a fair comparison because of the different hunting styles, but wolves kill only about eight percent of the animals they decide to hunt and coyotes even fewer.

It is as much a misconception to say that predators kill only the old,

The snarl of a cougar is defensive, not aggressive.

weak and sick as it is to say they wantonly slaughter far more than they need, just for the thrill of it. The single most important factors in prey selection are opportunity and hunger. Predators with "harass and test" hunting strategies, such as wolves and coyotes, probably do select more of the infirm. It's just easier to kill a weaker animal. But both wolves and coyotes are perfectly capable of killing healthy animals, and they sometimes do that, too.

Cougars, when hungry, kill whatever they encounter. But even without trying, they do take more mature bucks and fawns than other classes of deer. Both mature bucks and fawns tend to be vulnerable at times; fawns because of inexperience and bucks because of testosterone overload during the mating season. Bucks also are more active than other deer during the rut, exposing themselves to cougars more often. After the rut, bucks are emaciated and perhaps less alert than usual. During the rest of the year, bucks also tend to live in rougher country at higher elevations—perfect haunts for cougars. Bucks also tend to be more solitary compared to family groups of does and fawns, and they therefore have fewer eyes, ears and noses watching for potential trouble.

Nature's "wisdom," of course, says that males of many species are more expendable in the overall scheme, especially after they have mated. So, the cougar's unintended selection of buck deer helps to ensure that the overall food source doesn't shrink any more than necessary.

Above: Cougar cubs are weaned to solid food over their first six months.

Following pages: Fifty feet is the critical striking distance at the end of a cougar stalk.
This fawn has allowed the cougar too close.

Social Life

Cougar social life is nearly an oxymoronic concept; if it weren't for mating and cub-rearing, there would be no social interactions of cougars (and, of course, no cougars). Males will, on rare occasions, get together to fight and kill one another, but that example sounds more like anti-social interaction.

Scent-Marking

Residents of home ranges normally scrape-urinate to facilitate mutual avoidance, but the scrapes also may serve an opposite function when a female comes into her estrus period, or "heat." Cougar scientists are still in disagreement about whether females make scrapes at all, and if they do, how often. There is also no consensus about whether cougars scrape with their front paws or hind feet, or both. A male doesn't need a scrape to tell whether a female is in heat, he just needs a relatively fresh urine spot. He will then smell the spot in the flehmen posture, and decide whether to forgo the mutual avoidance philosophy, at least for a while. Females may use scrapes (discreetly, of course) to position them-selves for an encounter with a desirable male. They may also detect dif-ferences in desirability from the scrapes of males.

Although the cougar's sense of smell seems to us to be less important

Left: Social interactions between cougars are limited to mating and cub-rearing.

Following pages: Mating is an exhausting and sometimes noisy process.

than its vision and hearing, we humans operate from a position of disadvantage. Because our noses are so dulled, the only way we can make a guess at the meaning of a cougar scent activity is to associate it with behaviors immediately before and after the activity. What actually does go through a cat's brain at the time is a complete mystery.

Besides scraping, cougars perform other scent-marking activities. Sometimes a cougar will spray-urinate, purposely being messy. It could identify individuals to others, or the sex of the spraying cougar, or its sexual condition.

Cougars also stretch high and claw tree trunks. Other than possibly identifying individuals through either the height of the scratches or some secretion from interdigital glands, the meaning is unclear, at best. Cougars also rub their heads and necks on trees or rocks, spreading saliva and skin secretions on the object being rubbed. They could be identifying each other or taking care of an itch.

Another clue is that cougars do all of the aforementioned scent-marking at favorite sites, habitually. That could mean they are trying to get something across to other cougars, or it could mean that the smell from the last episode stimulates them to do it again. "What" is the easy question—"why" is the tough one.

When a cougar finds carrion, scat (cougar or other), vomit or even catnip or mint plants, there is a reasonable chance that it will roll in the material and rub its head and neck in it. Identification, sex, and condition are all possibilities for the meaning of this behavior.

Mating

The sexual politics of cougars are complicated by their reclusive behavior and tendencies toward mutual avoidance. Also, there is not a specific time of year for mating—females can come into heat at any time, but do so for only a few days each twenty-four-day cycle. Cougars are polygamous, so mating encounters of convenience are the rule. Probably because of the sparse distribution of both sexes, and possibly some territoriality in males, females rarely mate with more than one male.

Excess solitude can have an effect on cougars which is similar to humans. When it is finally time to mate, they make up for lost time.

Above: Amorous intentions are expressed in similar ways by many species.

Following pages: Occasionally, a young cub will wander off while its mother is away.

During this time, the male and female hunt together and sleep side by side. Although each coupling usually lasts less than a minute, cougars may copulate three times per hour for up to eight days. The couplings are accompanied by loud yowling, or caterwauling. I would image that unwary wilderness campers could be a bit unnerved by that much cat noise, that often.

Cougars are believed to have "induced ovulation," or fertility stimulated by special conditions. Most scientists attribute the frequency of cougar mating to the need for the female to be stimulated into ovulating. From an evolutionary perspective, it makes some sense that the female use some method to evaluate the vitality of males. If ovulation only happened after six or more days of constant mating, it would be a good test of the strength of a male. Considering how few times males and females come together, induced ovulation would maximize the chances of conception.

Raising Cubs

If conception does occur, the cougars go back to their hermit ways. The normal gestation period for a female is ninety-two days. She can have anywhere from one to six cubs (also called kittens), but the average is two to three. Two-year-old females that breed for the first time often have just one cub, which is not unusual for many other species. It is nature's way of ensuring that they break into the responsibilities of motherhood slowly. If all goes well, a female will breed every two years.

Cubs are born blind, weighing about a pound, and begin to nurse within an hour of birth. Their fur is covered with dark spots, for camouflage reasons, and they lose them gradually over their first two years of life. In the first two weeks, the cubs double their weight, their eyes and ears open, and they begin to explore their immediate environment. When the mother is gone on a hunt, cubs are vulnerable to other predators, including adult male cougars.

The "den" is usually a pile of brush, a talus slope of large boulders or a overhanging ledge. The mother will move the den to another site just about the time that the cubs are weaned, a little over two months. Moving cubs probably prevents eventual discovery (and subsequent cannibalism) by males. By weaning time they weigh close to ten

Above: Hunting its mother's leg or tail marks the beginning of a two-year apprenticeship for a cub.

Following pages: As cubs mature, their awareness of their environment expands.

A female will encourage cubs to hunt on their own.

pounds, and have their baby meat-eating teeth, which last until they are six months old.

Conventional wisdom says that the pounce and kill are instinctive behaviors in cougars, but selecting, stalking and burying the kill must be learned. Cubs, at two months, begin an apprenticeship which will last for at least a year. Female cougars have been observed training one-month-old cubs to catch grasshoppers. Early in the apprenticeship process, when the cubs are all eating directly from the kill, the kill site can be quite a mess. Three or more cubs hanging out in one eating spot for a few days will trample vegetation and spread bones out for a hundred feet around the carcass. Later, they will realize that concealing kills is in their best interest. Obviously, a deer carcass will be almost totally consumed in a couple of days by a family unit of three or four.

The probability that a cougar cub will survive through its first year is about seventy percent. A deer fawn's chances are around sixty percent. The difference between the two numbers, in part, reflects the quality of care given by female cougars. There is some preliminary evidence which suggests that cougars, in addition to suppressing their estrus cycle while they are raising young, can somehow give birth to the number of cubs a female can easily support. Some species of animals, like minks and weasels, can re-absorb embryos if conditions are harsh and raising young looks to be difficult. Cougars probably don't do it that way, but it does make some sense that the amount of stress on a female could affect her relative fertility. Even if this possibility proves untrue, the amount of prey certainly affects the number of cubs which survive to adulthood.

Although there has never been opportunity for humans to watch it happen, the mother cougar probably has to get assertive when it is time for the young to be off on their own. The young cougars have an instinct to disperse as well, but they know right where to find their mother within the home range, so she probably drives them off. It would be counter-productive for the entire population of cougars if young animals settled in the home area where they were born.

Dispersal

The life of a female cougar is a tough one. She spends a large share of that life providing for three or more, including herself. The life of a transient is also difficult. It spends its time hunting in unfamiliar territory, with marginal hunting skills, running the risk of an aggressive encounter with a resident cougar. The risk of dying is highest for newborns, transients and old adults—a mortality pattern common to many species.

There is often a ripple effect when transients are dispersing. Because the population of cougars is very lightly hunted in wilderness areas, they tend to live longer in those areas, and home ranges tend to be more stable. Stable adult populations and home ranges leads to higher reproduction rates, because only well-established adults breed. Vacancies in home ranges (through mortality) are uncommon, so dispersal of transients pushes them into areas peripheral to the wilderness, but still good deer and elk habitat. In these peripheral areas, the resident adults are hunted more, so there are more places for a transient to settle in and take over a good hunting range. If reproduction is high, because of good deer and elk populations in the wilderness, the transients may overload the periphery outside the wilderness, and the extra transients move into unsuitable habitat and/or agricultural areas. Those are the years when cougar predation on cattle and sheep tends to peak.

In my home area of central Idaho, for instance, winter severity is the major variable in the survival of deer and elk populations. It may seem logical that cougars will fare better when winters are easy, because the prey population remains high. Not so. An easy winter for deer and elk translates to harder-to-catch prey for cougars. During light winters, there is a predictable rise in the killing of domestic sheep, cattle and household pets by cougars.

Wilderness acts as a "seed" area for the overall cougar population, because the stability of the adult breeding population, the ratios of males to females, and the number of offspring is not affected to any degree by human predation on cougars. Wilderness also offers us a glimpse of the "normal" state of cougar affairs, the way it was before the rapid growth of our population. These places are a baseline from which we can measure our own effects on the world, and for that reason they

Above: Highly nocturnal cats have oval pupils. Cougar pupils are round, which gives a hint about their daily activity patterns.

Following pages: The presence of cougars helps define the presence of wilderness.

become extremely important to us, as well as cougars.

Maurice Hornocker, who most consider the "godfather" of cougar research, found that some transient cougars remaining in the wilderness areas after dispersal were still transients at five and six years of age. Probably, once upon a time in America when it was mostly wilderness, permanent homes were hard to come by for cougars; the resident population was stable. Today, human predation creates new openings every year.

Hornocker also found that old cougars can lose their home range to a rival younger animal and become transient again, completing one of many cycles in the life of a cougar. Nature is seldom kind, and almost never humane. That concept is an invention of ours, and we sometimes have a difficult time being consistent with that same ideal.

Cougars spend their middle adulthood in a routine. Mortality is very low (except when humans enter the equation) and they become efficient at providing for themselves and their cubs. They know their home well, and they have honed their survival skills. When they get to the ripe old age of ten, they again become vulnerable. At that age, chances are strong that they will lose a critical piece of equipment— their canine teeth. Teeth become more brittle after age ten, and sometimes one or both break off. Considering the importance of canine teeth in killing deer and elk, this is invariably a sentence of slow death. The cougar must then make a nearly impossible transition to existing on small game.

Cougar number 110 in Gary Power's study was a 15-year-old male of 180 pounds which had very recently broken all four canine teeth. Six months later, Power found it at a remote watering trough. It weighed 76 pounds. When a canine breaks off in an older animal, Power explained, it unbalances the stress on the remaining canines every time a killing bite is administered. The imbalance usually breaks off the other three canine teeth soon after.

Above: Cougars have a "digitigrade" stance, which means they move on their toes.

Following pages: A cougar stalk is mostly motionless, punctuated by short bursts of a few steps when prey is not watching.

chapter seven

The Human Factor

The future of cougars is enmeshed with their relationships to us. We are hunting them as a game animal, killing them on sight to prevent stock depredation, or giving them complete protection and trying to save remnant populations, depending on where we live. There is still widespread belief that cougars kill inordinate numbers of deer and elk, and can drive the populations of game species down to unhuntable numbers. Many ranchers feel that their very livelihood depends on eradicating cougars and other large predators.

But most of us, I would guess, are anything but firm in our opinions on cougars. We feel an ambivalence toward cougars which is natural, seeing them as majestic and dangerous at the same time. We are thrilled to spot one at a distance, but shudder to think of one less than fifty feet away, crouched, with its neck stretched forward.

So, we have our fears, but what is the reality?

When a deer hunter sees a buried cougar kill, it is easy to extend that single act by the cougar to the next level: cougars kill deer, therefore, more cougars means fewer deer. Many people don't carry the logic further. If they did, the next question would be "If that is true, and the cougars kill all the deer in an area, then what? The answer is, of course, that the cougars are doomed as well. Five million years of cougars eating deer does a bit of damage to this argument.

Although cougars sometimes resemble an African lion moving through savanna, they are very distant relatives.

Maurice Hornocker, in a ten-year study of radio-collared deer in the central Idaho wilderness, found that cougars had virtually no effect on deer numbers. He did find, however, that deer numbers had a huge effect on cougar populations. In other words, the amount of available prey completely dictated the numbers of predators which could eat them. Deer have a high reproductive potential, and a good third to half of them die each winter no matter what. Biologists call the number of prey species which will die anyway a "harvestable surplus." Deer create the "surplus" and cougars "harvest" them.

This is a fine distinction. What it means is that both populations, the predator and the prey, fluctuate together. But the fine point is that the prey population goes up or down first, and the predator population follows. In Hornocker's study, when the deer population went up, so did cougar populations. When the deer numbers went down, the cougar's did too. This has become almost an axiom among biologists who study predator-prey relationships—when a predator has a primary species of prey and is not flexible enough to switch to another species easily, the prey numbers will always dictate the numbers of predators.

So, no matter what, "those wolves," "those grizzlies" or "those cougars" are never going to eat all the deer and elk. It won't happen. It can't happen.

What can and does happen is this: Cougars do seem to have a tempering effect on wide fluctuations in the deer population, flattening the peaks and valleys; and cougars reduce competition for food among deer by eliminating some of them, therefore improving the condition of those which remain alive.

Livestock depredation by wild animals affects less than one percent of all farms and ranches each year. Although that doesn't sound like much, some of the unlucky ranchers can be affected significantly. What the facts of livestock depredation suggest is that "damage control" would be far more efficient (and cost-effective) if it were applied locally, in response to a real problem. In the past, animal damage control efforts have been applied in a "blanket" way, attempting to reduce predator populations overall, in the hopes that it would reduce the odds of any one rancher being affected. The poisoned meat set out to reduce overall predator populations left behind a lot of "collateral damage" as they say

Above: In the Everglades, wild hogs supplement the cougar's usual diet of deer.

Following pages: Winter fur gives a cougar a stocky appearance, an illusion only "hair deep."

*Cougar ears swivel independently, allowing them to listen
in several directions simultaneously.*

in wartime when innocent bystanders get killed.

The approach has also backfired with some species because of ignorance about their reproductive habits. It appears as though the hundred-year-war on coyotes has served to break up pack units, causing more coyotes to breed. The population of coyotes has exploded during the same time that millions have been killed, and their range in the United States has doubled. Things are never as simple as they seem.

The risk of a cougar attack, while still slight, has been increasing over the past twenty years. This is probably a function of more humans moving further into cougar country, and a corresponding increase in the number of cougars. There is a hot-spot of unpleasant cougar encounters—Vancouver Island in British Columbia. Almost forty percent of cougar attacks happen there. Speculation about the reasons centers around three things: the lack of some species of small prey, which forces poor-hunting yearling cougars to consider more options; the extremely thick cover on the island, preventing cougars from distinguishing between prey species until late in the stalk; and some genetic tendency in that subspecies which makes them bolder around humans.

Cougars rarely carry rabies. Only once has a cougar which attacked someone had a confirmed case of rabies (it happened in California, early this century). Two people died from the attack. They were not mortally hurt, but they died of the disease later. Considering the solitary nature of the puma, passing rabies from one animal to another would be difficult, so the rarity of rabies cases is assumed.

What possesses yearling cougars to attack humans? Because of their inexperience, they are probably hungrier than adults, and therefore less particular about their definition of "prey." But humans may have something to do with it, too. A puma's normal prey does not stand upright, and usually flees in an attempt at escape. What if you were, say, jogging (fleeing?) and stopped to tie a shoe (in the posture of a deer?). Could an inexperienced cougar make a mistake? That very scenario happened in the past few years at least twice, in Colorado and in California.

Nearly everyone who has turned toward the cougar at the time of attack and fought the cat has survived. As playing dead gives a grizzly attack victim a good chance at survival, fighting a cougar with all the ferocity a victim can muster will often make the cat see the error of its ways. Throw things, yell, wave arms, swing sticks—if the extremely unlikely ever happens. Don't, under any circumstances, run. Running switches cougar brains to instinctive autopilot, and the fastest human will not outrun the slowest cougar.

Even though cougar attacks are rare, the perception of aggression is enhanced by the big cat's typical feline curiosity. A number of times, cougars have been caught in the act of "stalking" humans as they walk along a trail. When discovered, they flee, but that fact doesn't seem to reassure our species. If it is any consolation, they probably follow us far more often than we know. It is their job to keep it a secret.

The mortality statistics are far greater when prey and predator reverse roles. Humans have probably killed somewhere between 100,000 and 250,000 cougars since Columbus arrived. We viewed cougars as an enemy, to be sure, but the elimination of cougars from their eastern range was more a function of growing human population than an all-out war on cougars. Higher human population densities meant more encounters and more casual opportunity for those humans with guns. In less populated areas, even bounty programs had little over-all effect on cougar populations, because there were just too few bounty hunters to keep up with the reproductive potential of the cougar. In Idaho, for instance, eighty cougars per year were killed during the boun-ty years. Today, sport hunting with dogs takes about 350 per year. The number of cougars killed is carefully monitored, as well as ratios between young and adult, and male and female cougars.

Among the states with a still viable cougar population, most take a middle-of-the-road approach to human-caused cougar mortality. On the ends of the spectrum, California has a complete ban on cougar killing and Texas still sees them as vermin, placing no limits on the take. Cougar hunting is, like all hunting, controversial. But the furor over the question of hunting ignores the real cause of the decline in the cougar's range. Cougars need space, and humans take it. If the cougar is to have any chance of survival over the long run, we two-leggeds must curb our appetite for land.

What is the cougar's future? Is it just a continuation of the trends of the past? Or, have we learned enough to ensure its survival through management techniques?

The shorter and narrower management views count cougars, deer, elk and hunters, throws them into a yearly equation, and decides how

Cougars are remarkably free of parasites, possibly (in part)
because of their personal hygiene.

A cougar's low, wide crouch allows it to freeze in any position.

many of each come out the other end of the formula. It is true that there are so many of us humans that we must be considered in the management schemes of cougar biologists. What we tend to forget, however, is that the cougar doesn't need us. No wildlife does, for that matter. They were here long before we were even here, let alone developing management schemes.

What the cougar needs is land. It needs space. Given enough space, cougars, deer, elk, grizzlies and wolves will dance to the symphony of the ecological process. It is a process we did not invent. We only named it, and only recently, at that. In an ideal cougar world, there would be ample roadless areas to seed the general population. There would be relatively wild corridors between those roadless areas, to foster the movement of transients and to mix genes for the long-term greater good. If these things were done, in the cougar ideal world, the rest would take care of itself.

Not surprisingly, those who know the cougar best fear it the least. John Beecham is one of those biologists who gets a twinkle in his eye when the subject turns to cougars. He told me of a time when he and Gary Power were trying to get radio collars on cougars. It was late in the day, and the tracking hounds were finally making their "we've got one treed" sound from about three miles across a steep canyon. Beecham and Power looked at each other, because of the late hour, nodded an unspoken agreement, and started running down the canyon wall toward the sound. Beecham describes Power, who stands far over six feet, as an "animal" when there's climbing to do. Power literally ran all the way down and then all the way back up the other side of the canyon, to get there before dark. When Beecham finally arrived at the treed cougar, Power was coughing blood with a big grin on his face. They darted the cat just at dark, but didn't have enough light to process and measure, to get the data they needed. Power slung the cougar over his shoulders and they brought it to his house. There, on the living room floor, they took blood, weighed, checked teeth—all the things they had no light for in the woods. The cougar spent the night there at Power's house, with Power re-administering tranquilizers every so often, and his wife warily watching the "house guest" out of the corner of her eye.

In the morning, they brought the cougar back to where they had treed it, and let it go with a new necklace. If Beecham's story is a good one, imagine the one that cougar could tell.

Power also tells of a time when he pieced together, from tracks in the snow, an encounter between a cougar and a porcupine. The cougar was moving downstream in a narrow creek bed, and the porcupine upstream. The tracks clearly showed where the cougar had first spotted the porcupine and stopped. As the porcupine continued to amble upstream, the cougar slid to the side and waited in ambush behind a stump. The tracks showed the pounce, and the cougar landing directly in front of the porcupine. But the porcupine tracks just ended. There was absolutely no struggle, just a spot of blood and an empty porcupine skin. "That speaks a volume on the way a cougar hunts," said Power. "Killing efficiently is critical with a porcupine. You get messy, you pay."

In fact, the only time Power has ever felt threatened by a cougar had to do with porcupine quills. He treed an old female with broken canines. It was thin, and had been feeding on marginal food, as evidenced by the quills in its nose and mouth. Power climbed up an adjacent tree to get an eye-level picture of the cat before he tranquilized her for processing. She growled and turned toward him, defensively coiling for a leap. At that point, Power realized that the distance between his tree and hers was not far enough. Nothing transpired, as was usual for his cougar encounters, but he did have a bit more adrenaline in his blood for a while.

People who work with cougars have noticed an encouraging shift in public perception of the big cat. Hound hunters will just as often shoot with a camera these days. Cougars are a protected species in every state except Texas. Their populations are increasing almost everywhere west of the prairies. Today, a ranch kid will brag to a buddy at school that he saw a cougar. Twenty years ago, the story would have been about shooting it. Watching wildlife has become mainstream big business, and the chance of seeing a cougar, or even a track, still raises hair on our necks, but for entirely different reasons.

The mystery of cougars continues to intrigue the curious. We want to know more about them than they let us see. Someday, we may see the cougar in an entirely different way. It is now the subject of study. But someday, when we come full circle in our attitudes about land and wildlife, the cougar will probably be seen as a teacher.

Above: Cougars are both shy and curious.

Following pages: Cougar—the majestic enigma.

Selected Reading List

Ackerman, D. *A Natural History of the Senses*. New York: Random House, 1990.

Anderson, A. *A Critical Review of Literature on Puma* (Felis Concolor). Colorado Department of Wildlife, Spec. Rep. 54, 1983.

Banfield, W. *The Mammals of Canada*. Toronto: University of Toronto Press, 1974.

Braun, C., Ed. *Mountain Lion—Human Interaction*. Proc. of the Symposium and Workshop, Colorado Division of Wildlife, Denver, 1991.

Hemker, T., B. Lindzey and B. Ackerman. "Population characteristics and movement patterns of cougars in southern Utah." *Journal of Wildlife Management* 48 (1984): 1275-1284.

Hornocker, M. "An analysis of mountain lion predation upon mule deer and elk in the Idaho Primitive Area." *Wildlife Monographs* 21 (1970): 1-39.

──────. "Winter territoriality in mountain lions." *Journal of Wildlife Management* 33 (1969): 457-464.

McBride, R. "Status and ecology of the mountain lion *Felis concolor stanleyana* of the Texas-Mexico border." Master's thesis, Sul Ross State University, Alpine, Texas, 1976.

Seidensticker, J., et al. "Mountain lion social organization in the Idaho Primitive Area." *Wildlife Monographs* 35 (1973).

Shaw, H. *Mountain Field Guide*. Special Report 9, Arizona Game and Fish Dept., 1987.

Smith, A. *Ute Tales*. Salt Lake City: University of Utah Press, 1992.

Sweanor, L. "Mountain lion social organization in a desert environment." Master's thesis, University of Idaho, Moscow, 1976.

Van Dyke, F., et al. "Reactions of mountain lions to logging and human activity." *Journal of Wildlife Management* 50 (1986): 95-102.

Wright, B. *The Eastern Panther—A Question of Survival*. Toronto: Clarke, Irwin & Co., 1972.